EXPEDITION
TO THE
GALÁPAGOS ISLANDS

To: Leo, Cora, and Ryan

Grayson Rigby

Explore!

EXPEDITION
TO THE
GALÁPAGOS ISLANDS

GRAYSON RIGBY

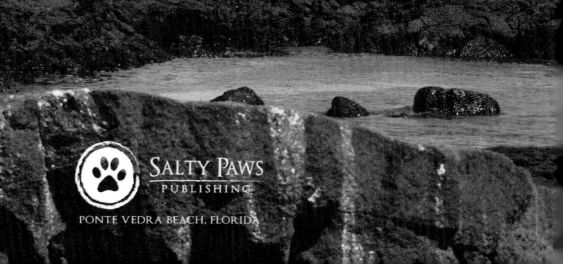

SALTY PAWS
PUBLISHING

PONTE VEDRA BEACH, FLORIDA

Book and cover design by Sagaponack Books & Design

Map design by KM Creative Designs

Back cover wave created by Freepik

Editing by Mansbridge Editing & Transcription

Photographs by Grayson Rigby and Gary Rigby

Illustrations by Grayson Rigby

ISBN:

978-0-9986680-0-0 (softcover)

978-0-9986680-1-7 (ebook)

978-0-9986680-2-4 (hardcover)

Library of Congress Control Number: 2017937816

Summary: An eight-year-old adventurer traveling aboard the *National Geographic Endeavour* explores the Galápagos Islands and shares his experiences and encounters with the endemic animals.

JNF058000 Juvenile Nonfiction / Travel

JNF003000 Juvenile Nonfiction / Animals

TRV010000 Travel / Essays & Travelogues

TRV024040 Travel / South America / Ecuador & Galápagos Islands

TRV011000 Travel / Special Interest / Family

TRV001000 Travel / Special Interest / Adventure

Printed and bound in the United States of America
First Edition

Dedicated to my parents,
who encourage me to be adventurous.

*The world is a book, and those who do not
travel read only a page.*
—Saint Augustine

ACKNOWLEDGMENTS

Thank you to all the naturalists on the ship *National Geographic Endeavour*, for teaching me interesting facts about the Galápagos Islands and its endemic animals.

My mom was a big help and inspiration in this project, and encouraged me to follow my dream of being an author.

PREFACE

Expedition to the Galápagos Islands is a travel journal that I originally wrote in my eight-year-old voice. Now, at 11, I have recently added: Why Are the Galápagos Islands So Special?; Animal Facts; a glossary; and some illustrations.

Introduction

My name is Grayson Rigby and I am eight years old. I live on a barrier island in Northeast Florida and I am in the third grade. I am going to share with you my experiences about my first expedition to the Galápagos Islands, Ecuador, on the ship the *National Geographic Endeavour*. The Galápagos Islands has been my favorite trip yet, because of all the amazing and neat animals that I saw, such as sea lions, land iguanas, marine iguanas, birds, fish, sea turtles, and tortoises.

Endemic Animals in the Galápagos

One of the first things I learned from the naturalists on the *National Geographic Endeavour* is that the word *galápago* is Spanish for "tortoise." The islands were named after the Galápagos giant tortoise. I also learned about all of the endemic animals that live in the archipelago. *Endemic* means that the animals are found only in one place, like the Galápagos Islands and nowhere else in the world.

Galápagos Sea Lion

I went hiking on the island of North Seymour, and there were sea lions everywhere! They were on the rocks, on the path where we were walking, and in the water. I saw a newborn baby sea lion, which was black and slimy. I was very lucky to see it.

Magnificent Frigatebird

I also saw a lot of nesting magnificent frigatebirds. The male magnificent frigatebird has a red pouch, or gular sac, on their chest that they blow up to impress the females. I almost fell over with laughter because the male frigatebirds were making a sound like a drum with their pouch, to get the females' attention and attract a mate.

Male and female frigatebirds.

An interesting fact about frigatebirds is that they are the biggest crooks of all birds. Sometimes they steal food and nesting twigs from other birds so they can eat and make a home without doing the work.

Frigate babies are fluffy and white.

Juvenile frigatebird napping.

Flightless Cormorant

I live in the state of Florida, and our cormorants can fly. But in the Galápagos, the flightless cormorant cannot fly because of their tiny wings. Although they cannot fly, they are excellent swimmers and divers due to their large webbed feet.

During one of my snorkeling excursions, a flightless cormorant went after a fish and was inches from my face! I was very surprised because I didn't see the bird until he was right in front of me.

This flightless cormorant is sitting on a nest and caring for a baby.

Blue-Footed Booby

Blue-footed boobies are an unusual-looking bird because of their blue feet and blue beaks. They are great divers and swimmers like the flightless cormorants, because they also have webbed feet.

I saw a blue-footed booby dancing ... he was trying to get a mate. The male gives the female twigs for the nest and tries to impress her by showing off his feathers and blue feet and by making whistling sounds. If she likes him, she makes a honking sound.

Galápagos Land Iguana

This is a male Galápagos land iguana. I know he is a male because of his large size and the spines on the crest of his head. He is sunning to get warm since he is a cold-blooded reptile.

I saw land iguanas eating cactus as a source of food and water.

Galápagos Marine Iguana

While visiting Punta Espinoza on Fernandina Island, I climbed black lava flows and rocks and saw lots and lots of marine iguanas. They were all huddled together on the lava rocks, sunning. The special thing about marine iguanas is that they are the only lizards in the world that swim.

Marine iguanas eat algae from the lava rocks while completely underwater. When they are eating algae they drink a lot of salt water, so when they get back on shore they blow the salt out of their noses.

They reminded me of dragons because of their scaly bodies and the spikes on their back, but obviously without the fire breathing and wings. Instead, they were hacking, coughing, and snorting all over the lava flows.

Galápagos Penguin

While snorkeling at Punta Vicente Roca, Isabela Island, I saw three Galápagos penguins. They kept nipping at each other in the water and if one got too close to another they snapped their beaks at the other.

The Galápagos penguin is one of the smallest penguin species in the world and is endemic to the Galápagos Islands. This penguin only breeds in a tropical climate along the equator.

Short-Finned Pilot Whale and Bottlenose Dolphin

I saw short-finned pilot whales and bottlenose dolphins hunting for squid and fish together! I counted five babies in the whale pod and about 20 adults. After watching them for a while, we went to the lounge inside the ship and when I looked out the window, I saw a dolphin jumping all the way out of the water. It was great!

Galápagos Giant Tortoise

We visited the Charles Darwin Research Station at the Galápagos National Park Service on the island of Santa Cruz. I learned about how baby tortoises grow and how researchers collect the tortoise eggs from different islands in the Galápagos archipelago. The scientists bring back the eggs to the research facility and put them in incubators to hatch. When the babies hatch, they are separated in enclosures, according to their age and the island they came from. As they grow, their carapace, or shell, gets harder. When they are old enough to fend for themselves, they can be released into the wild again.

When I saw the tortoises for the first time, I couldn't believe how big they were. I wondered how they could get so big from being so small when they were babies. In addition, I could not believe that some of them were more than 100 years old. Since I am now eight, I figure they have been on Earth at least 92 years longer than I have.

While on a hike, I saw two tortoises in the wild. One was younger and the other was an adult. The smaller tortoise was about the size of a wheelbarrow and the older one was slightly larger than a bathtub.

Galápagos Sea Lion Pup

We went to Punta Pitt, on the easternmost island called Isla de San Cristóbal. When we were on the red sand beach, we saw a sea lion pup. Our naturalist guide said the sea lion was about two to three weeks old. I waited patiently, and it came right up to me and sniffed my knee. I had a funny feeling when the whiskers started tickling my skin and it made me laugh. Seeing the baby sea lion was the best thing of all for me!

Red-Footed Booby

After visiting with the baby sea lion, we hiked up into the mountains. The hike was difficult and challenging because it was a steep, dry riverbed covered with lava rocks. While hiking we saw frigatebirds, Nazca boobies, and red-footed boobies. When we got back down to the beach, I swam in the ocean and, later, built a sand castle.

Whitetip Reef Shark

On our last day in the Galápagos Islands we went snorkeling at Kicker Rock. Kicker Rock is two big rocks— the size of skyscrapers—that look like they are exploding out of the ocean. When we were snorkeling I saw whitetip reef sharks, sea turtles, and big schools of fish. When I saw the sharks, I really wanted to swim down right next to them and see what it would be like to be a whitetip reef shark.

Favorite Animal in the Galápagos

The first time that I saw a baby sea lion, it was hard not to pick it up and hug it because the sea lion was so cute. When I looked at the sea lions playing, they made me feel overjoyed.

One of my favorite experiences with sea lions was when they were swimming with me while I was snorkeling. I was watching my favorite fish, the streamer hogfish, when a baby sea lion came at me at full speed.

Just when I thought it was going to smash into me, it came to a complete stop and blew a spray of bubbles at my face. When the bubbles came in contact with my face, they popped on my cheeks and I felt a tickling sensation. I started laughing in my snorkel, and when I popped up for air the sea lion swam like a rocket straight through my legs!

Sea Lions
A Poem by Grayson Rigby

Sea lions, sea lions,

Very playful, as you see.

Splashing, flipping, swimming around.

What fun it would be to be a sea lion!

WHERE IN THE WORLD ARE THE GALÁPAGOS ISLANDS?

London

New York

Los Angeles

Galápagos
Islands

Equator

Rio de Janeiro

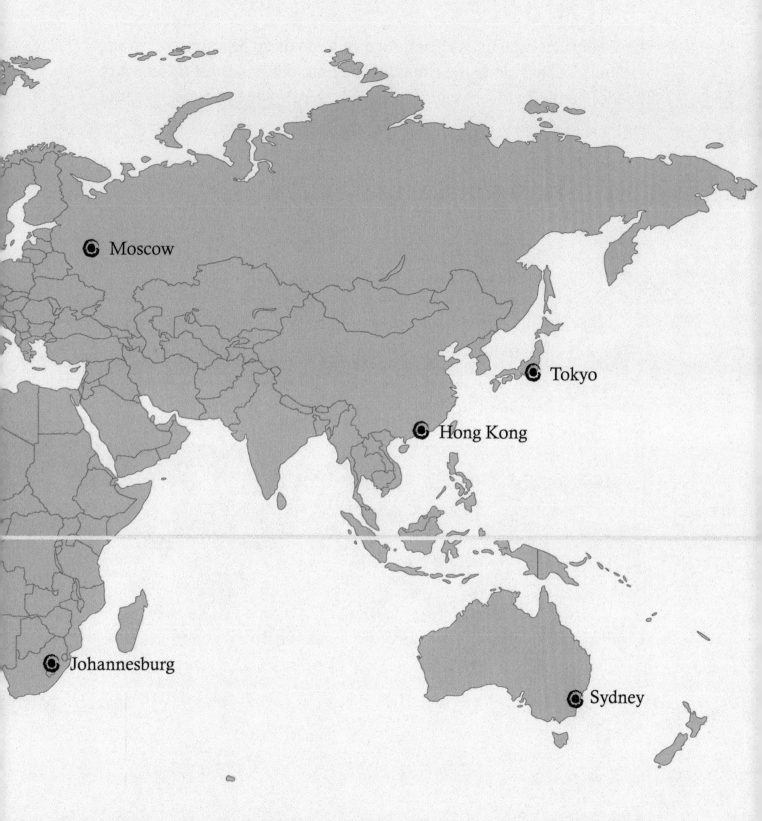

Moscow

Tokyo

Hong Kong

Johannesburg

Sydney

WHY ARE THE GALÁPAGOS ISLANDS SO SPECIAL?

The Galápagos Islands are composed of a small archipelago, or group, of islands located along the equator. They are 600 miles off the coast of Ecuador, in the Pacific Ocean. The islands were made by volcanoes about 6 million years ago.

It took a few million years for plants and animals to inhabit the islands. Scientists believe that plants on the mainland dropped seeds that drifted to the islands, where they grew. Also, the wind carried seeds to the archipelago and to higher places on the islands.

The animals arrived in different ways. For instance: birds flew to the islands; fish and ocean mammals swam and were probably pushed by the strong ocean currents; and land animals used tangled vegetation rafts as well as the currents to get to the archipelago.

Today, people inhabit 3% of the Galápagos Islands and 97% is preserved as a national park.

The Galápagos Marine Reserve is one of the largest reserves in the world. More than 50,000 square miles of water surrounding the archipelago are protected against fishing and hunting.

ANIMAL FACTS

Blue-Footed Booby: One characteristic of the blue-footed booby is that it nests on the ground. The female lays two or three eggs. Unlike other birds, the booby does not have a brooding pouch, which is the warm area under a bird that incubates the eggs. Instead they use their big, blue webbed feet, which have an increased amount of blood flow and make the feet warm. After the egg hatches, the chick sits on top of the mother's feet for a month to keep warm. The blue-footed booby gets its food by plunge-diving into the ocean and catching fish in its beak.

Bottlenose Dolphin: Bottlenose dolphins live in tropical to subtropical water. Dolphins are carnivores and eat squid and fish. After 12 months of pregnancy, a female dolphin gives birth to one calf. The calf stays with the mother for one and a half to two years. Other female bottlenose dolphins within the pod also care for the baby. Bottlenose dolphins communicate by using a unique personal whistle that tells their location and how they are feeling. Calves that are only one month old have the ability to whistle.

Flightless Cormorant: The female flightless cormorant lays eggs in a nest on the ground near the shore. The bird makes the nest out of seaweed and other random objects. When the chicks hatch, both parents take turns caring for the hatchlings. Later, the male takes over and cares for the chicks. These birds dive deep into the ocean to catch eels and other fish, and octopus for food.

The flightless cormorant does not have many predators. As a result, over time their wings have gotten smaller. However, their bodies have become bigger and heavier so they can dive and catch fish easily.

A change that takes place over time is called evolution. Evolution helps animals and plants thrive in their environment.

The flightless cormorant is on the vulnerable species list due to El Niño and invasive species.

Galápagos Giant Tortoise: The Galápagos giant tortoise can live up to 200 years. They spend 16 hours a day sleeping and resting. Tortoises are herbivores and eat cactus, grasses, and native fruit. Females lay about 10 eggs in a nest that is buried in the ground. When the eggs hatch, the tortoises have to survive on their own. Females return to the same nesting spot every breeding season.

The Galápagos giant tortoise almost became extinct because humans were using them as a food source. During the 1800s, whalers, merchant sailors, and pirates came to the Galápagos. They discovered that the giant tortoise doesn't need food or water for up to a year. As a result, the sailors stored the tortoises on their ships so they could have fresh meat during their journeys.

Another reason that the tortoise nearly became extinct is because of invasive species like goats, pigs, dogs, and cats. These animals came to the Galápagos by traveling on ships from other countries. People brought the animals to the archipelago and set them free. Goats ate the same plants as the tortoises and destroyed the tortoises' food source. Since then, the goats have been eliminated from the islands. Predators such as dogs and cats eat tortoise eggs.

The Galápagos giant tortoise is on the endangered species list because of invasive species.

Galápagos Land Iguana: Land iguanas use their enormous claws to dig burrows in the ground so they can keep warm at night. The female land iguana lays about 25 soft-shelled eggs in a burrow which is buried under moist sand and decomposed leaves. Galápagos land iguanas are mostly herbivores and eat prickly pear cactus leaves and native fruits. The males are territorial when other iguanas step onto their doorstep.

The land iguana is on the vulnerable species list because of invasive species.

Galápagos Lava Lizard: The Galápagos lava lizard is commonly seen throughout the archipelago. At night they bury themselves in the dirt. The female lays from one to four eggs underground. Male lava lizards do "push-ups" to attract female mates and to intimidate other males. They change their skin color according to their mood. These lizards are omnivores because they eat insects, arthropods, and cactus.

Magnificent Frigatebird: The magnificent frigatebird has a long bill that they use to carefully collect fish from the ocean. The frigatebird has to be careful because it cannot get wet, or else it will drown. The bird's feathers don't have the oil needed to make a waterproof coat on its body, which would act like a rain slicker.

Also, frigatebird nests are made of twigs and are close to the ground, in shrubs and thickets. Frigatebirds lay only one egg each breeding season. The parents both incubate the egg and later care for the hatchling for up to six months.

Galápagos Marine Iguana: Marine iguana males defend breeding territories while female marine iguanas lay from one to six eggs in a burrow buried in volcanic ash or sand. Their long flat tail is excellent for swimming, and they feed on marine algae underwater.

The marine iguana is on the vulnerable species list because of invasive species.

Galápagos Penguin: The Galápagos penguin mates for life, and the female lays two eggs in nests found in little caves that are inside cliffs along the waterline. For about one month after the eggs hatch, both parents take turns protecting and caring for the chicks.

Scientists are trying to increase the penguin population by making artificial nests. The reason the penguin population is low is because their fish supply is dropping and invasive predators have become a problem. Galápagos penguins are carnivores and eat small fish and marine invertebrates.

The Galápagos penguin is on the endangered species list.

Red-Footed Booby: The red-footed booby is the smallest of the boobies. They nest in trees and shrubs and lay only one egg. Like the blue booby, the red-footed booby also stands on the egg and warms it with their feet. They go on long hunting trips with other boobies to catch flying fish and squid.

Sally Lightfoot Crab: The Sally Lightfoot crab lives on rocks along the shoreline, just above the spray point. The females have a clutch of eggs that vary from 20 to 100, depending on the female's size. The female carries the eggs on her underbelly, and when it's time for the eggs to hatch she rubs her belly on a rock over shallow water to remove the eggs. Once they hatch, the larvae eat phytoplankton and must survive on their own.

Sally Lightfoot crabs are omnivores and scavengers because they will eat just about anything that they can get their claws on. The crabs use their claws to scrape food off rocks, as well as catch live animals such as fish and mollusks.

Galápagos Sea Lion: The Galápagos sea lion is social, playful, and energetic. They communicate with one another by barking. Females give birth to one pup each breeding season. A few days after the pups are born, the mothers hunt for fish and leave their babies on the beach or in shallow-water nurseries. When the

babies are about five months old they learn how to catch fish on their own. Baby sea lions stay with their mothers for about one to three years. When they are not fishing or playing, they spend long hours lying on the beach in the sun.

The Galápagos sea lion is on the endangered species list due to El Niño and invasive species.

Short-Finned Pilot Whale: Short-finned pilot whales live in tropical to subtropical deep water. Pilot whales are black with white-gray markings on their throat and chest, and have bulging foreheads. They are carnivores and eat squid, octopus, and fish. After 15 months of pregnancy, female pilot whales give birth to one calf. The mother cares for the baby whale for two years. If the calf is a male it leaves the pod, but if it is a female it stays with the pod. The other females help to raise the calf and look after the baby when the mother is hunting for food.

They communicate with one another by whistling, clicking, slapping their tails on the surface of the water, and breaching (jumping out of the water).

Swallow-Tailed Gull: The swallow-tailed gull is the only nocturnal gull in the world. They hunt mostly at night and eat squid and fish. The gulls' large eyes help them see well at night. During breeding season, they have a red outer ring around the eye. Gulls nest on rocky slopes and ledges near the beach. The female lays one egg, and both parents incubate the egg and later care for the fledgling.

They are nearly endemic—found only in one other place other than the Galápagos Islands.

Whitetip Reef Shark: The whitetip reef shark is gray with a white tip on its dorsal fin and tail fin. A unique feature of the whitetip reef shark is that they can lie still for hours on the sea floor. Other sharks have to stay in motion to breathe, but the reef shark does not. During the day, the shark stays in caves with other reef sharks—stacked like logs. This nocturnal reef shark waits for nighttime to hunt. They are carnivores and eat octopus, crabs, and sleeping fish that are in the crevices of coral reefs. The female has up to five pups.

The whitetip reef shark is on the near-threatened species list.

GLOSSARY

archipelago: A group of islands.

arthropods: Species such as spiders, insects, centipedes, shrimp, krill, and more. They have a segmented body, jointed legs, an external skeleton or armor, and are cold blooded.

carapace: The hard shell of a tortoise, turtle, crustacean (crab, shrimp, lobster), or arachnid (spider, scorpion, tick).

carnivore: An animal that eats meat.

El Niño: Every two to seven years, weather conditions warm the ocean off the coast of Ecuador and Peru. This warming of the ocean causes coral reefs, algae, and phytoplankton to die. In addition, the water is too warm for fish and they die or travel to cooler waters. Birds, marine mammals, and reptiles lose their food sources and suffer.

endangered: A species that is at risk of becoming extinct.

endemic: An animal or plant that is native to a particular country, island, or area; for example: the endemic plants and animals that are found only in the Galápagos Islands and nowhere else in the world.

equator: An imaginary line around the earth that equally divides the northern and southern hemispheres.

evolution: When a species changes over time in order to live better in its environment.

expedition: A journey or voyage by a group of people for the purpose of exploration and scientific discovery.

extinct: A species that is no longer in existence.

fledgling: A young bird that has grown feathers and is learning how to fly.

gular: The throat of an animal, especially a bird, fish, or reptile.

herbivore: An animal that eats plants.

incubate: To sit on eggs to warm them so they will hatch.

incubator: A box used to hatch eggs artificially. The temperature and humidity can be controlled to provide an ideal environment for the eggs.

invasive species: Animals or plants that are not native to an ecosystem and cause harm to the native plants and animals that live there.

invertebrate: An animal that does not have a backbone, which includes most of the animals in the world.

mollusk: Animal with a soft body, which usually lives in a shell, such as a snail or a clam.

naturalist: A person who studies animals and plants in their natural surroundings; a wildlife expert, scientist, or expert of natural history.

omnivore: An animal that eats both plants and meat.

phytoplankton: Microscopic marine plants that provide food for a wide range of sea animals.

predator: An animal that preys on or hunts other animals.

scavenger: An animal that eats dead animals and plants.

INDEX

RESOURCES

For additional information about the endemic and unique animals found in the Galápagos Islands, visit the following online resources:

 Galápagos Conservancy

 Charles Darwin Foundation

 Animal Diversity Web

 *National Geographic Kids*

  International Union for Conservation of Nature

 Salty Paws Publishing

GIVING BACK TO THE GALÁPAGOS ISLANDS

Grayson Rigby is a partner with the Galápagos Conservancy. A portion of the proceeds of each book sold is donated to the Conservancy to assist in research, conservation management, and education in the archipelago.

The Galápagos Conservancy is a highly rated nonprofit organization that works closely with the leadership of the Galápagos National Park, Charles Darwin Research Station, and the Government of Ecuador. Their experts and scientists are working to conserve, protect, and restore the fragile ecosystem of the Galápagos Islands for future generations to enjoy.

FROM THE AUTHOR

My name is Grayson Rigby and I love to travel and explore new places all over the world. In my free time, I enjoy outdoor sports, drawing, creating comics, and collecting books. My biggest inspiration has to be my love of reading. I read genres of all kinds including fantasy, science fiction, mysteries, and more. All of this reading has inspired me to follow my dreams of becoming an author and illustrator, and I encourage you to follow your dreams too.

Grayson at eight years old in the Galápagos Islands.

ABOUT THE AUTHOR

At the age of eight, Grayson went on a family vacation to the Galápagos Islands. He was inspired by the incredible animals and wrote daily in his journal about his observations and personal experiences.

The following year, at the age of nine, Grayson won the Lindblad Expeditions-National Geographic Young Explorer Challenge for his journal, *My First Expedition to the Galápagos Islands*. Lindblad Expeditions-National Geographic honored Grayson with a complimentary expedition to Seattle, Washington, and the San Juan Islands aboard the *National Geographic Sea Lion*.

When Grayson was 10, he won first place in the St. Johns County School History Essay Contest for his paper titled "Exploration, Encounter, and Exchange," an essay about Ft. Mose and Captain Francisco Menendez.

He is currently 11 years old and in fifth grade. Grayson serves as a Student Ambassador at his elementary school, reads to shelter animals through the Pawsitive Reading program at the Humane Society, and participates in a variety of community service projects.

Grayson is looking forward to attending middle school and continuing his studies. He is also planning his next expedition and eagerly anticipating a new adventure. Grayson lives with his parents and goldendoodle Ellie on a barrier island in Northeast Florida.

Keep in touch with Salty Paws Publishing for more great books by author Grayson Rigby.

Grayson at 11 years old.

CPSIA information can be obtained
at www.ICGtesting.com
Printed in the USA
FSOW03n0402111017
39739FS